50 *Novelty* PARTY CAKES FOR CHILDREN

50 *Novelty* PARTY CAKES FOR CHILDREN

FUN AND FANTASY DESIGNS FOR EVERY CELEBRATION

SUE MAGGS

LORENZ BOOKS

This edition is published by Lorenz Books, an imprint of Anness Publishing Ltd,
Blaby Road, Wigston, Leicestershire LE18 4SE;
info@anness.com

www.lorenzbooks.com; www.annesspublishing.com

If you like the images in this book and would like to investigate using them for publishing, promotions or advertising, please visit our website www.practicalpictures.com for more information.

Publisher: Joanna Lorenz
Editor: Gillian Haslam
Jacket Designer: Nigel Partridge
Photographer: Edward Allwright
Production controller: Mai-Ling Collyer

For all recipes, quantities are given in both metric and imperial measures, and where appropriate, measures are also given in standard cups and spoons. Follow one set, but not a mixture, because they are not interchangeable.

PUBLISHER'S NOTE
Although the advice and information in this book are believed to be accurate and true at the time of going to press, neither the authors nor the publisher can accept any legal responsibility or liability for any errors or omissions that may have been made nor for any inaccuracies nor for any loss, harm or injury that comes about from following instructions or advice in this book.

Contents

Introduction

A novelty cake is the perfect way to celebrate a child's birthday, family celebration or other special event, and can form the focal point of a particular party theme, to reflect hobbies, toys and activities. To make things easier for cooks who are not experienced cake-makers, all of the cakes in this book are based on square or round sponge cakes. Many are ideal for busy parents, who want to create something special but don't have the time or expertise to produce labour-intensive icing effects. Many of the designs are quite simple, and are

Above: This gift-wrapped parcel cake is simple to make but looks very attractive with its vibrant ribbons.

embellished and enhanced with candies and small decorations – the children will love the additional treats, and can save the decorations as mementos of their special day. The cakes can also be made a few days ahead of the party, and as long as they are covered with fondant and stored in a cool place, they can be worked on gradually, whenever the time is convenient.

A useful section at the front of the book provides all you need to know about the necessary equipment, such as piping tubes and cutters, cake decorations and candles. As well as the basic cake recipes, there are instructions about how to line a cake tin, make a glaze, prepare marzipan, make various types of icing and add edible colouring. Step-by-step pictures show how easy it is to make your own piping bags and how to use them.

Of the 50 cake decorating ideas – ranging from pirate hats and a paddling pool to fairy castles and a cat in a basket – there will be something to appeal to children of all ages, and you won't have to spend precious hours in the kitchen to achieve fantastic results. Delight your friends and family with a glorious cake and make every children's party or celebration an instant success!

Right: Fondant icing has been used to great effect in this fun cake of a cute mouse in bed.

Equipment

Some specialist tools are useful for icing and decorating cakes, but generally you will have most items in your kitchen.

weighing scales

cake tins

serrated knives

Cake boards
Silver cake boards are perfect for finished cakes. They come in circles, squares and rectangles from 10cm/4in to 30cm/12in in diameter.

Cake tins
All the cakes in this book use round or square tins. 15cm/6in, 20cm/8in and 25cm/10in are the most useful.

Electric hand-held beaters
Essential for making cake batters and icings.

Icing smoother
This will give a uniform finish to fondant-covered cakes.

Measuring spoons
These are available in both metric and imperial measurements. Always measure level unless otherwise stated.

Mixing bowls
A set of various sizes is useful for mixing cake batters and icings.

Palette knives
Use for spreading butter icing onto cakes.

Pastry brush
This is essential for greasing cake tins, and brushing cakes with apricot glaze.

Plastic chopping board
Use this as a smooth, flat surface to roll out fondant icing.

Plastic scrapers
These can be used to create 'combed' patterns in butter icing.

Rolling pin
Use a heavy pin for rolling out marzipan and fondant.

Round pastry cutters
A set of cutters in various sizes can be used to create perfect rounds of fondant for decoration.

Sable paint brushes
These are used for fine details on cakes.

Serrated knives
Sharp knives with a serrated edge will allow you to cut cakes without breaking.

Sieves
Used for sifting flour into cake mixtures, and icing sugar to prevent lumps. Smaller sieves can be used to sift icing sugar onto a work top when rolling out fondant.

Turntable
This enables you to turn the cake as you decorate which makes the task simpler.

Weighing scales
Used for weighing ingredients for cakes.

Wooden cocktail sticks (toothpicks)
Use to make designs on cakes, or to support pieces of cake to make a shape. Always remove them before serving.

mixing bowls

sieves

cake tins

rolling pin

turntable

wooden spoons

measuring spoons

round pastry cutters

electric hand-held beaters

sieve

palette knives

wooden cocktail sticks

plastic chopping board

sable paint brushes

pastry brush

plastic scrapers

icing smoother

cake boards

Cake Decorations

Specialist cake decorating shops will stock a variety of appealing items that can be used to enhance cakes. They range from sugar mice and candles to various types of colours and tints.

Cutters
These include a daisy flower cutter, a holly leaf cutter and a small flower cutter, all used for cutting fondant shapes for decoration. Metal cutters can be purchased from specialist cake decorating shops and kitchenware suppliers.

Candles
A wide variety of shapes and colours are available from party shops.

Candle holders
These are made of plastic, and come in various colours and sizes.

Edible paste colours
These are very concentrated, so use sparingly. They can be kneaded thoroughly into fondants to produce a uniform colour. To avoid staining your hands, wear latex gloves when mixing colours into icing.

Flower cutters with ejectors
These can be bought singly or in a boxed set with a small round sponge, and come in 5mm/¼in, 8mm/³⁄₈in and 1cm/½in sizes. The ejector is on a spring, and the icing flowers are pressed out of the cutter on to the sponge, to both shape and mould them simultaneously. They can be bought from specialist cake decorating shops and kitchenware suppliers.

Metal piping tubes
These are a good investment so it is worth buying the best quality as they will produce lovely icing effects and will last for years. The most useful ones to buy initially to start your collection are the no. 22 basket weave tube (a flat tube with a serrated edge); no. 1 writing tube (for writing, drawing outlines and producing run-outs); nos. 7 and 8 star tubes and no. 44 scroll tube for piping borders. They are available from both specialist suppliers and party shops.

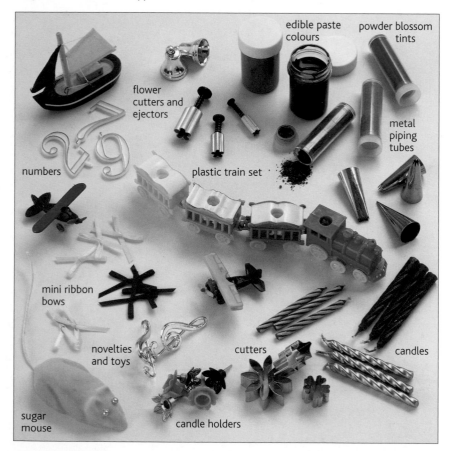

numbers

flower cutters and ejectors

edible paste colours

powder blossom tints

metal piping tubes

plastic train set

mini ribbon bows

novelties and toys

cutters

candles

sugar mouse

candle holders

Left: A range of delightful decorations and equipment to enhance cakes. Specialist shops will carry a variety of items, but toy shops also carry small toys and novelties.

Mini ribbon bows

These are delightful additions to cakes and can be purchased in a large variety of colours. Simply stick them into icing.

Novelties and toys

You are likely to find a novelty to reflect almost any theme you wish in the better cake decorating shops. Illustrated here are plastic treble clefs, plastic miniature aeroplanes and plastic silver bells. The wooden sailing boat was purchased from a toy shop, another good source of small toys and novelties.

Plastic train set

This can also hold candles. The carriages are detachable so the correct number of candles may be used.

Powder blossom tints

These are edible dusting powders which come in various colours, and are used for brushing onto fondant icing to produce subtle shading. They can also be mixed to a paste with a product called rejuvenator, and then painted directly onto fondant like paints. Both products are available from specialist cake decorating shops.

Sugar mice

These examples are home-made, and were made in plastic moulds with string tails, but sugar animals can also be purchased from specialist confectioners.

Lining a Cake Tin

Lining tins is important so that the cakes come out of the tin without breaking or sticking to the base of the tin. This method is simple, but essential.

1 Place the tin on a piece of greaseproof paper, draw around the base with a pencil and cut out the paper inside this line.

2 Grease the base and sides of the tin with melted lard or soft margarine and stick the piece of paper in neatly. Grease the paper. It is now ready for filling.

Apricot Glaze

This is used to seal the cake and stop the crumbs working their way into the icing. It will also stick the marzipan or fondant to the cake.

Ingredients
175g/6oz/½ cup apricot jam
15ml/1 tbsp water

1 Gently heat the apricot jam in a pan with the water, then use a wooden spoon to rub the jam through a sieve to remove any lumps. Return to the pan and heat until boiling before brushing carefully over the cake.

Basic Recipes

This useful chart provides quantities to make three sizes of cake, either round or square shapes, with corresponding amounts of butter icing for each size.

The recipes in this book all use simple round or square cake shapes. Make up the cake to the required size, according to the chart on these pages.

For the lightest sponge cakes, use soft unsalted butter or margarine. They can be used straight from the fridge so all the ingredients can be put in a bowl and whisked together as there is no need to cream the fat and sugar first.

BUTTER ICING

To make up the required amounts of buttercream icing, use the amount of icing (confectioner's) sugar specified for the total weight of icing (350g/12oz/2¾ cups butter icing requires 350g/12oz/2¾ cups icing (confectioner's) sugar). Consult the chart to establish the proportions of unsalted butter and milk required for the required amount of icing (confectioner's) sugar.

FONDANT, MARZIPAN AND ROYAL ICING

Where a recipe calls for fondant icing, you can use shop-bought fondant icing to save time, or make your own. For fondant, the total weight of fondant required is equal to the amount of sugar used. Likewise, marzipan can be shop bought, or you can make the marzipan recipe in larger or smaller quantities. You can buy royal icing or use the royal icing recipe, which can be made in smaller or larger batches: the sugar used is equal to the total weight called for in the recipe.

BASIC SPONGE CAKE AND BUTTERCREAM

15cm/6in round cake:
2 eggs
115g/4oz/½ cup caster (superfine) sugar
115g/4oz/½ cup butter or margarine
115g/4oz/1 cup self-raising (self-rising) flour
2.5ml/½ tsp baking powder
15ml/1 tbsp water

Butter icing:
15g/½ oz/1 tbsp butter
7.5 ml/1½ tsp milk
50 g/2 oz/½ cup icing sugar, sifted

Baking time:
35–45 minutes

15cm/6in square cake:
3 eggs
175g/6oz/¾ cup caster (superfine) sugar
175g/6oz/½ cup butter or margarine
175g/6oz/1½ cups self-raising flour
4ml/¾ tsp baking powder
30ml/2 tbsp water

Butter icing:
15g/½oz/1 tbsp butter
7.5ml/1½ tsp milk
50g/2oz/½ cup icing sugar, sifted

Baking time:
45–55 minutes

20cm/8in round cake:
3 eggs
175g/6oz/¾ cup caster (superfine) sugar
175g/6oz/¾ cup butter or margarine
175g/6oz/1½ cups self-raising (self-rising) flour
4ml/¾ tsp baking powder
30ml/2 tbsp water

Butter icing:
25 g/1 oz/2 tbsp butter
15 ml/1 tbsp milk
115 g/4 oz/1 cup icing sugar, sifted

Baking time:
45–55 minutes

20cm/8in square cake
4 eggs
225g/8oz/1 cup caster (superfine) sugar
225g/8oz/1 cup butter or margarine
225g/8oz/2 cups self-raising flour
5ml/1 tsp baking powder
45ml/3 tbsp water

Butter icing:
25g/1oz/2 tbsp butter
15ml/1 tbsp milk
115g/4oz/1 cup icing sugar, sifted

Baking time:
50–60 minutes

25cm/10in round cake
6 eggs
350g/12oz/1½ cups caster (superfine) sugar
350g/12oz/1½ cups butter or margarine
350g/12oz/3 cups self-raising (self-rising) flour
7.5ml/1½ tsp baking powder
75ml/5 tbsp water

Butter icing:
50g/2oz/¼ cup butter
30ml/2 tbsp milk
225g/8oz/1½ cups icing sugar, sifted

Baking time:
1–1¼ hours

25cm/10in square cake
8 eggs
450g/1lb/2 cups caster (superfine) sugar
450g/1lb/2 cups butter or margarine
450g/1lb/4 cups self-raising flour
10ml/2 tsp baking powder
105ml/7 tbsp water

Butter icing:
50g/2oz/¼ cup butter
30ml/2 tbsp milk
250g/8oz/2 cups icing sugar, sifted

Baking time:
1½–1¾ hours

Basic Sponge Cake

All the cakes in this book are based on basic sponge cakes. Consult the chart opposite for the correct proportions needed, and follow the simple steps below.

1 Preheat the oven to 190°C/375°F/ Gas 5. To grease and base line the cake tins, trace around the base of the tin you will be using on greaseproof paper and cut out the circle. Grease the inside of the tin lightly with melted butter or margarine, then press the greaseproof paper onto the bottom of the tin.

2 Put the eggs, sugar, margarine and flour into a bowl. Measure the baking powder level with a knife and add to the bowl.

3 With an electric whisk, mix all the ingredients together until the mixture is smooth and light.

4 Spoon the cake mixture into the prepared tin. Spread it evenly to the sides of the tin and smooth the top before baking.

5 Bake the sponge cake in the centre of the oven for about 25 minutes to 1 hour for the largest size, or until a thin skewer inserted into the cake comes out clean. Loosen the sides carefully with a knife.

6 Cover a wire cooling rack with a piece of greaseproof paper (this will prevent the cake from sticking) and turn the cake onto the rack. Cool completely before cutting, using or storing.

TO MAKE BUTTER ICING

1 Soften the butter, add the milk and the icing (confectioner's) sugar.

2 Beat the ingredients together. Add any flavouring and colouring.

COOK'S TIPS

Citrus Butter Icing: beat in 5ml/1 tsp finely grated lemon or orange rind to the basic recipe.
Fruity Butter Icing: mix in 15ml/1 tbsp fresh raspberry purée or juice.

Marzipan

All the cakes are covered with a layer of marzipan. This seals in the moisture and gives the cake a smooth, flat surface, which is much easier to ice. Marzipan is easy to work with and useful for modelling. If your children do not like the taste of marzipan, then just replace it with a layer of fondant.

Ingredients
225g/8oz/2 cups ground almonds
275g/10oz/1¼ cups caster
   (superfine) sugar
175g/6oz/1¼ cups icing
   (confectioner's) sugar
1 egg
15–30 ml/1–2 tbsp lemon juice
3 ml/½ tsp almond extract

1 Mix all the dry ingredients in a bowl. Whisk the egg with the lemon juice and almond extract and add this to the almond and sugars in the bowl.

2 Mix to form a paste. Wrap in clear film and keep in the refrigerator up to a week until needed. Roll out on a work surface dusted with a little sifted icing sugar.

Royal Icing

This is used for piping, run-outs and sticking decorations onto cakes. It dries very hard and holds its shape when piped.

Ingredients
1 large egg white
225g/8oz/1½ cups icing (confectioner's)
   sugar, sifted

COOK'S TIPS
Dried egg white powder is available from supermarkets. It is whisked together with water and sifted icing (confectioner's) sugar, following the instructions on the packet. It, too, must be covered at all times, as it dries very quickly.
Keep icing in the refrigerator in an airtight container for up to a week. It will separate out and will need remixing before use. You may have to add icing sugar to thicken it.

1 Whisk the egg white in a large bowl with a fork. Add a quarter of the icing sugar and beat well.

2 Work in the icing sugar, beating well between each addition until the mixture holds its shape. Lay a piece of clear film on top of the icing and cover the bowl with a damp cloth to prevent the icing drying out. Store at room temperature.

Quick Fondant Icing

This can be bought or home-made. It is soft and pliable and must be worked with fairly quickly, as it will dry out. It should be wrapped securely in clear film if you are not using it. Roll out on a smooth work surface dusted with a little sifted icing sugar or cornflour. It remains fairly soft for cutting and eating.

Ingredients
500g/18oz/3¼ cups icing (confectioner's)
    sugar, sifted
1 large egg white
30ml/2 tbsp liquid glucose (clear
    corn syrup)

COLOUR EFFECTS
Different effects can be achieved by applying the colours not only with a soft brush but on a sponge. A pale wash of colour can be painted on the icing and allowed to dry, then a fairly dry brush can be dragged across to give a 'woodgrain' effect.

1 Put the icing sugar, egg white and glucose into a food processor or mixer and blend together until the mixture resembles fine breadcrumbs.

2 Knead the mixture until smooth and pliable. Add a drop of water if it is too dry. A little cornflour may be added to prevent it becoming sticky.

Gelatine Fondant Icing

This type of fondant icing is used for fine moulding decorations as it dries very hard.

Ingredients
60ml/4 tbsp water
15g/½oz powdered gelatine
10ml/2 tsp liquid glucose (clear
    corn syrup)
500g/18oz/3¼ cups icing (confectioner's)
    sugar, sifted

COLOURING FONDANT
Specialist cake decorating shops sell a wide range of colours. Only thick paste colours must be used to colour the fondant; liquid colours make it too wet. Knead into the ready-made fondant. Coloured lustre powders can be brushed on after the icing has dried.

1 Put the water in a heatproof bowl and sprinkle on the gelatine. Soak for 2 minutes. Place in a pan of hot, not boiling water, and stir until the gelatine dissolves and is clear. Remove from the pan, and stir in the glucose. Stir to cool slightly.

2 Put the sifted icing sugar into a bowl and mix in the gelatine mixture. Add more icing sugar or cornflour if the mixture is too wet, or a little water if it is too dry. Knead until smooth and pliable, and wrap in clear film until needed.

Making a Greaseproof Paper Piping Bag

Piping bags for icing are simple to make at home. Make one for each colouring you will need.

1 Cut greaseproof (waxed) paper into 25cm/ 10in square. Fold in half diagonally to make a triangle. Fold again to mark the centre of the folded edge.

2 Then, holding the centre, roll one point of the triangle up to the central line and the other point around that to make a tight cone.

3 Fold the edges over to secure the top of the bag.

Using a Piping Bag

Using a piping bag takes a little practice initially. It's best to try a few sample designs first.

  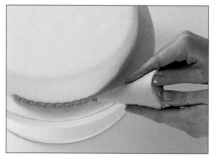

1 Cut off the tip, insert a piping tube and half-fill with royal icing.

2 Push the icing down well and fold both corners of the bag over to secure. Fold the top edge down several times until the icing is tightly packed in the bag.

3 Hold the bag in one hand and pipe in an upright position, guiding the bag with the other hand.

Making Run-outs

Run-outs can be piped onto the cake or onto greaseproof paper which has been secured with masking tape to keep it crease-free. Draw shapes onto the paper then pipe the outlines, then flood them to form a slightly domed surface.

1 Pipe the outline with No. I writing tube, following the marks on the greaseproof paper. Slacken the icing with a drop of water but don't make it too runny or it will overflow the sides; though if it is too thick, it will not give a smooth surface.

2 Half-fill a greaseproof piping bag with soft icing, snip off the tip and fill the outline shape generously to make the surface slightly domed. Use a pin to coax the icing into difficult areas and to break bubbles when they appear on the surface.

3 Allow the run-outs to dry for at least 48 hours before peeling away the paper. Stick on the cake with a little royal icing.

COOK'S TIPS

Always use freshly made icing. The correct consistency of the icing for 'flooding' should collapse and lose its shape if the bowl is tapped.

Making and Using Templates

Templates are a useful way of transferring a design from a book or drawing onto the surface of a cake. There are some designs, letters and numbers at the back of the book to use.

1 Place tracing or greaseproof paper over the design to be copied and, using a sharp pencil, outline it neatly.

2 Turn the paper over and outline the design on the underside. Turn the tracing the right way up and draw over again until a faint outline shows on the cake.

3 Now the design can be piped over the outline to cover any marks.

COOK'S TIPS

• If tracing a name, first draw a straight line on the paper with a ruler so that all the letters are even.
• A more laborious method is pricking the design through the paper straight onto the cake with a pin.

Cat in a Basket

The pretty woven pattern of the basket is quite simple to do but is surprisingly realistic. If you cannot model a cat from marzipan then use a toy or suitable ornament.

15cm/6in round cake
50g/2oz/¼ cup butter icing
350g/12oz/2¼ cups pink marzipan
225g/8oz/1½ cups green marzipan
225g/8oz/1½ cups yellow marzipan
50g/2oz/¼ cup white fondant
apricot glaze
food colourings: red, green, yellow
    and brown

Equipment
20cm/8in round cake board
fine paint brush

1 Split and fill the cake with butter icing. Place on the cake board. Measure the circumference of the cake with string, fold in half and measure (this will give the length of the marzipan strips to be cut). Brush with hot apricot glaze.

COOK'S TIP
Don't overwork the marzipan because it may become sticky. Dusting your hands with cornflour can help prevent it sticking. Marzipan can be coloured using pastes, but the colour will be slightly muted.

2 Roll out the pink marzipan to a 35 x 46cm/14 x 18in rectangle. Cut into five 1cm/½in strips, long enough to fit half way round the cake, about 25cm/10in. Cut the green marzipan into 7.5cm/3in lengths of the same width. Fold back alternate pink strips and lay a green strip across widthways. Fold back the pink strips over the green strip to form the weave, fold back the second lot of pink strips and repeat the process. Press lightly to join.

3 Press the basket weave around the sides of cake, joining the sides neatly.

4 Model a yellow cat about 7.5cm/3in across. Leave to dry overnight.

5 Roll out the fondant and place onto the cake and arrange in folds around the cat. Trim the edges.

6 Roll out any leftover pink and green marzipan into long ropes. Twist together and lay around the edge of the basket then press on neatly. With a fine paint brush and brown colouring, paint the face and markings on the cat.

Bella Bunny

This is a simple cake that would be suitable for very young children. The decoration is easy, the icing is spread over the cake and does not require any special techniques.

2 x 15cm/6in round cakes
350g/12oz/2¼ cups butter icing
apricot glaze
115g/4oz/2 cups desiccated coconut (dry unsweetened shredded)
50g/2oz/¼ cup white fondant
food colourings: red and brown
marshmallows

Equipment
25 x 35.5cm/10 x 14in cake board
6 wooden cocktail sticks (toothpicks), stained brown with food colouring
candles

1 Split and fill the cakes with butter icing. Cut a 10cm/4in circle out of one cake and place both cakes on the cake board.

2 Round off any sharp edges. Use the trimmings to make the ears and feet.

3 Brush all the pieces of cake with hot apricot glaze. Cover with the remaining butter icing then cover with coconut, pressing on lightly.

4 Colour a piece of fondant pink and roll and shape the nose. Cut out oval shapes for the ears and put into place. Colour a small piece of fondant brown, roll two small balls for the eyes and put into place with the nose.

5 Stick cocktail sticks on either side of nose for whiskers. Push the candles into the marshmallows and place on the board around the cake. Decorate around the cake with coloured ribbons, if wished.

Pink Monkey

This cheeky little monkey can be made in any colour fondant you wish. Once you have covered the cake with fondant icing, store in a cool place until the cake is required.

20cm/8in round cake
115g/4oz/¾ cup butter icing
apricot glaze
450g/1lb/3 cups marzipan
450g/1lb/3 cups pink fondant
50g/2oz/¼ cup white fondant
food colourings: pink, blue and black

Equipment
25cm/10in round cake board
candles

1 Split and fill the cake with butter icing. Place on the cake board and with a sharp serrated knife, use the template to cut out the basic shape of the monkey. Use the trimmings to shape the nose and tummy. Brush with hot apricot glaze and cover with a layer of marzipan then pink fondant. Leave to dry overnight.

COOK'S TIPS
Because fondant icing dries out easily, it is best to work quickly. If you have to stop working on it, cover it with clear film or plastic to avoid drying out. Cool your hands before working on the icing.

2 Mark the position of the paws and face. Colour a little of the fondant blue, roll out and cut out the eyes. Colour a little fondant black and cut out the pupils and tie.

3 Colour the remaining fondant pink and cut out the paws, nose, mouth and ears. Stick the features in place with water. Roll the trimmings into two balls and place on the board for the candles.

Mouse in Bed

This cake is suitable for any younger child. The duvet and sheets may reflect their favourite colour. Make the mouse well ahead to allow it time to dry.

20cm/8in square cake
115g/4oz/¾ cup butter icing
apricot glaze
450g/1lb/3 cups marzipan
675g/1½lb/3 cups fondant
food colourings: blue and pink

Equipment
25cm/10in square cake board
edible food colour pens: pink and blue
flower cutter

1 Split and fill the cake with butter icing. Cut 5cm/2in off one side and reserve; the cake should measure 20 x 15cm/8 x 6in. Place on the cake board and brush with hot apricot glaze. Cover with a layer of marzipan. With the reserved cake, cut a pillow to fit the bed and cover with marzipan, pressing a hollow in the middle for the head. Cut a mound for the body and legs of the mouse and cover with marzipan. Leave to dry overnight.

2 Cover the cake and pillow with white fondant. Lightly press a fork around the edge to make a frill around the pillow. Roll out 350g/12oz/2¼ cups of fondant and cut into 7.5cm/3in wide strips. Dampen around the edge of the bed and drape the valance around.

3 To make the top sheet and quilt; colour 75g/3oz/½ cup of fondant blue and roll out to an 18cm/7in square to cover the bed. Lightly mark a diamond pattern with the back of a knife and press a flower cutter into the diamonds to mark. Put the pillow and body on top of the cake and cover with the quilt.

4 Roll out a little white fondant and cut a 2.5 x 19cm/1 x 7½in strip for the sheet, mark along one length to resemble a seam and place over the quilt, tucking it in at the top edge.

5 Colour 25g/1oz/2 tbsp of marzipan pink and make the head and paws of the mouse.

6 Put the mouse into bed with the paws over the edge of the sheet. Draw facial markings onto the mouse with edible food colour pens.

Spider's Web

Make the spider several days before you need the cake to allow it to dry. The consistency of the glacé icing has to be right; practise by pouring the icing onto a baking tray and piping on the web.

20cm/8in round cake
225g/8oz/1½ cups butter icing
apricot glaze
30ml/1 tbsp cocoa
chocolate vermicelli
40g/1½oz/4 tbsp yellow marzipan
food colourings: red and brown
225g/8oz/1½ cups icing
    (confectioner's) sugar

Equipment
25cm/10in round cake board
wooden cocktail stick (toothpick)
star tube
candles

1 Split and fill the cake with half the butter icing. Brush the sides with hot apricot glaze. Add the cocoa to the remaining butter icing then smooth a little over the sides of the cake. Roll the sides of the cake in the chocolate vermicelli and place on the cake board.

2 To make the spider, roll 25g/1oz/2 tbsp of the yellow marzipan into two balls for the body and thorax. Colour a small piece of marzipan red and roll into small dots, then stick them onto the back. Divide the rest of the marzipan into eight pieces and roll into legs 5cm/2in long. Stick into place and leave to dry on greaseproof (waxed) paper. Make brown eyes and a red mouth and stick in place.

3 Make the spider's web. The glacé icing sets quickly, so have everything at hand. Sift the icing sugar into a bowl, then gradually beat in 15–30ml/1–2 tbsp water. Place the bowl in a pan with hot, not boiling, water. Heat gently and stir the icing; it should coat the back of the spoon. If the icing is too thick add a drop of water and if it is too thin add a little sifted icing sugar. (Do not overheat the icing.) Remove from the pan, dry the bowl and quickly pour two-thirds of the icing over the top of the cake. Spread to the edges with a palette knife. Tap the cake on the work surface to flatten the icing.

4 Add a drop of brown colouring to the remaining icing and pour into a piping bag. Snip off the end to form a tiny hole and pipe concentric circles onto the cake, starting from the centre and working outward. With a cocktail stick, draw across the cake from the centre outward, dividing it into quarters. Then draw them from the edge of the cake inward, dividing it into eighths. Leave to set.

5 Put the rest of the chocolate butter icing into a piping bag fitted with a star tube and pipe a border around the edge of the web. Put candles evenly around the border and the spider in the centre.

Teddy's Birthday

After all the pieces have been assembled and stuck into the cake with a little water, an icing smoother is very useful to flatten the design.

2 Colour one-third of the remaining fondant pale brown. Colour a piece pink, a piece red, some blue and a tiny piece black. Using a template, cut out the pieces and place in position on the cake. Stick down by lifting the edges carefully and brushing the undersides with a little water. Roll small ovals for the eyes and stick in place with the nose and eyebrows. Cut out a mouth and press flat.

20cm/8in round cake
115g/4oz/¾ cup butter icing
apricot glaze
350g/12oz/2¼ cups marzipan
450g/1lb/3 cups white fondant
food colourings: brown, red, blue
   and black
115g/4oz/¾ cup royal icing
silver balls

Equipment
25cm/10in round cake board
No. 7 star tube
No. 7 shell tube
1.5m/1¾ yards 2.5cm/1in wide ribbon
candles

1 Split and fill the cake with butter icing. Place on the cake board and brush with hot apricot glaze. Cover with a layer of marzipan then fondant. Using a template, mark the design on top of the cake.

3 Tie the ribbon around the cake. Colour the royal icing blue and pipe around the base of the cake with the shell tube and tiny stars on the small cake with the star tube, inserting silver balls. Add the candles.

Party Teddy

There is very little piping needed on this cake, only the teddy's features have to be piped. The teddy is built up with royal icing and coloured coconut.

20cm/8in square cake
115g/4oz/¾ cup butter icing
apricot glaze
450g/1lb/3 cups marzipan
350g/12oz/2¼ cups white fondant
25g/1oz/½ cup desiccated coconut
food colourings: blue and black
115g/4oz/¾ cup royal icing

Equipment
25cm/10in square cake board
small bow
candles

1 Split and fill the cake with butter icing. Place on the cake board and brush with hot apricot glaze. Cover with a thin layer of marzipan then white fondant. Leave to dry overnight. Using a template, carefully mark position of the teddy onto the cake.

VARIATION
Change the colour as required; for a girl, a pink body with pale pink paws and brown features and a brown ribbon is an option.

2 Put the coconut into a bowl and mix in a drop of blue colouring to colour it pale blue. Spread a thin layer of royal icing within the lines and before it dries, sprinkle some pale blue coconut over the icing and press down lightly.

3 Roll out the fondant trimmings and cut out nose, ears and paws. Stick in place with a little royal icing. Tie the ribbon round the cake. Colour a little royal icing black and pipe on eyes, nose and mouth. Pipe a white border around the base.

Hickory Dickory Dock

This appealing cake is based on the nursery rhyme. Small children love the jolly clockface, and the sugar mouse can be given as a prize.

20cm/8in round cake
15cm/6in square cake
225g/8oz/1½ cups butter icing
apricot glaze
675g/1½lb/4½ cups marzipan
450g/1lb/3 cups brown fondant
115g/4oz/¾ cup white fondant
food colourings: brown, gold, red, blue
    and black
2 silver balls
50g/2oz/¼ cup royal icing

Equipment
25 x 36cm/10 x 14in cake board
10cm/4in piece of string
no. 1 writing tube

1 Split and fill the cakes with butter icing. Cut two wedges off one end of the square cake 6cm/2½in from the corner.

2 Use a cake tin as a guide to cut a semi-circle from the opposite end of the square cake to fit around the round cake. Place on the cake board and brush with hot apricot glaze. Cover with a layer of marzipan then brown fondant.

3 Roll out half the white fondant and cut a 15cm/6in circle for the face and a window for the pendulum. Cut out a 5cm/2in long pendulum and 5cm/2in and 6cm/2½in long hands.

4 Paint the pendulum and hands gold and leave to dry overnight.

COOK'S TIP
You may want to model extra mice from pink fondant for the children to take home at the end of the party.

5 Colour most of the remaining fondant pink and make a mouse with a string tail and silver balls for eyes. Leave to dry overnight on greaseproof paper.

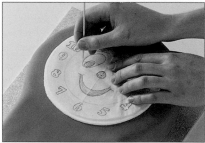

6 Stick on the clock face with water. Using a template, mark the numbers and face on the clock. Colour the royal icing black and pipe the numbers with a no. I tube. Stick on with water. Roll out the excess brown fondant and edge the face and the window. Colour the remaining fondant blue, red and black. Roll out and cut the eyes, pupils, eyebrows, mouth and centre. Stick on the hands, features, pendulum and mouse with a little water.

Noah's Ark

This cake is decorated with small animals, about 4cm/1½in high, available from party and cake decorating shops. Children will love to take home one of the novelties, as a reminder of the party.

20cm/8in square cake
115g/4oz/¾ cup butter icing
apricot glaze
450g/1lb/3 cups marzipan
450g/1lb/3 cups light brown fondant
115g/4oz/¾ cup royal icing
food colourings: brown, yellow and blue
chocolate mint stick

Equipment
25cm/10in square cake board
rice paper flag
small animal cake ornaments

1 Split and fill the cake with butter icing. Cut a rectangle 20 x 13cm/8 x 5in and cut to shape the hull of the boat. Place diagonally on the cake board.

2 Cut a smaller rectangle 10 x 6cm/ 4 x 2½in for the cabin and a triangular roof from the remaining piece of cake. Sandwich together with buttercream or apricot glaze.

3 Cover the three pieces with a layer of marzipan then cover the hull and cabin with brown fondant. Sandwich together with butter icing and place in position on the hull. Make a long roll from the remaining brown fondant and stick round the edge of the hull with a little water. Mark planks of wood with the back of a knife. Leave to dry overnight.

4 Colour one-third of the royal icing yellow and spread over the roof with a palette knife. Roughen it with a skewer to look like thatch.

5 Colour the remaining royal icing blue and spread over the cake board, making rough waves. Stick a rice paper flag onto the chocolate mint stick and press on the back of the boat. Arrange the small animals around the deck of the boat. Stick them onto the boat with a dab of butter icing.

Bumble Bee

This friendly bee is very effective, but quick and simple to construct. The edible sugar flowers may be bought ready-made, but these ones were made specially, and are very easy to make.

20cm/8in round cake
115g/4oz/¾ cup butter icing
apricot glaze
350g/12oz/2¼ cups marzipan
350g/12oz/2¼ cups yellow fondant
115g/4oz/¾ cup black fondant
50g/2oz/¼ cup white fondant
food colourings: yellow, black, blue, red and green
115g/4oz/¾ cup royal icing
50g/2oz/½ cup desiccated coconut

Equipment
25cm/10in square cake board
1 paper doiley, cut in half
sticky tape
1 pipe cleaner

1 Split and fill the cake with butter icing. Cut in half, sandwich both halves together and stand upright on the cake board. Trim the ends to shape the head and tail. Brush with warm apricot glaze and cover with marzipan then a layer of yellow fondant.

2 Roll out the black fondant and cut out three stripes 2.5 x 25cm/1 x 10in. Leave about 10cm/4in for the head from the end of the cake and stick the stripes evenly spaced behind the head with a little water. Roll out and cut eyes from the fondant. Colour a little fondant blue, roll out and cut two eyes. Colour a little fondant yellow and set aside. Colour the remainder pink and cut out a mouth.

3 Stick on the features with water. To make the daisies, cut out six 2.5cm/1in rounds from pink fondant and stick a small ball of yellow in the centre of each. Cut the petals with a knife and mark the flower centres with a cocktail stick.

4 Mix the coconut with green colouring. Cover the cake board with royal icing then sprinkle over the coconut. Add the daisies. For the wings, wrap each doiley half into a cone shape and secure with sticky tape. Cut the pipe cleaner in half and stick into the cake behind the head. Place the wings over the pipe cleaners.

Horse Stencil

Remember to use a fairly dry brush when painting the design on the cake and allow each colour to dry completely before adding another.

20cm/8in round cake
115g/4oz/¾ cup butter icing
apricot glaze
450g/1lb/3 cups marzipan
450g/1lb/3 cups yellow fondant
food colourings: yellow, brown, black,
   red, orange and blue

Equipment
25cm/10in round cake board
fine paint brush
child's stencils
1¼m/1¾ yards ribbon
candles

1 Split and fill the cake with butter icing. Place on the cake board and brush with warm apricot glaze. Cover with a layer of marzipan then yellow fondant. With the leftover fondant, roll into two thin ropes, long enough to go half way round the cake. Brush the lower edge of cake with a thin band of water. Lay the fondant around the cake and press the joins together. Make pattern in the border with the decorative handle of a spoon. Leave to dry overnight.

2 If you do not have a stencil, make one by tracing a simple design onto a thin piece of card, then cut out the shape with a sharp knife. Place the stencil of the horse in the centre of the cake. With a fairly dry brush (do not use the brush too wet or the colour will run under the stencil), gently brush over the parts you want to colour first. Allow these to dry completely before adding another colour, otherwise the colours will run into each other. Clean the stencil between colours.

3 Complete the picture then paint on the lettering. Tie the ribbon around the sides of the cake and place the candles on top.

Magic Hat

Children will love this cheery little character bursting from a top hat; it's a perfect centrepiece, and will set the scene for a magic theme party.

2 x 15cm/6in round cakes
225g/8oz/1½ cups butter icing
115g/4oz/¾ cup royal icing
apricot glaze
450g/1lb/3 cups marzipan
675g/1½lb/4½ cups grey fondant
225g/8oz/1½ cups pink marzipan
food colourings: black and pink
silver balls

Equipment
25cm/10in square cake board
1.5m/1¾ yards pink ribbon

1 Split and fill the cakes with butter icing, then sandwich them one on top of the other. Stick on the centre of the cake board with a little royal icing. Brush with hot apricot glaze. Cover with a thin layer of marzipan then with grey fondant. Roll out the remaining fondant to a 20cm/8in round. Cut a 15cm/6in circle from the centre, and lower carefully over the cake. Shape the sides and hold in place to dry.

2 With the remaining grey fondant, roll out to a 15cm/6in circle, cut a cross in the centre, place on the hat and curl triangles over a spoon to shape. Smooth the join around the edge of the hat.

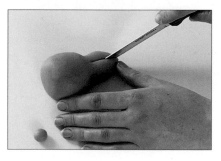

3 Shape the rabbit's head with pink marzipan, about 5cm/2in in diameter, shaping a slightly pointed face. Mark the position of the eyes, nose and mouth. Shape the ears around the handle of a wooden spoon and leave to dry separately overnight.

4 Stick the rabbit in the centre of the hat with a little royal icing. Tie the ribbon round the hat. Pipe a border of royal icing around the top and base of the hat and decorate with silver balls while the icing is still wet.

5 Colour the remaining royal icing black and pipe the eyes and mouth.

COOK'S TIP
For a softer royal icing that will not set too hard, beat 5ml/1 tsp glycerine into the mixture. Glycerine is sold bottled in liquid form in pharmacies and larger supermarkets.

Treasure Chest

Allow yourself a few days before the party to make this cake. The lock and handles are made separately, then left to dry for 48 hours before sticking onto the cake.

20cm/8in square cake
115g/4oz/¾ cup butter icing
apricot glaze
350g/12oz/2¼ cups marzipan
350g/12oz/2¼ cups brown fondant
50g/2oz/1 cup desiccated coconut
115g/4oz/¾ cup royal icing
food colourings: brown, green and black
edible gold dusting powder
25g/1oz/3 tbsp white fondant
silver balls
chocolate money

Equipment
30cm/12in round cake board

1 Split and fill the cake with butter icing. Cut the cake in half and sandwich the halves on top of each other. Place on the cake board.

VARIATION
Citrus butter icing: Instead of the milk, add orange or lemon juice and the grated rind of half of the fruit.

2 Cut the top to shape the rounded lid and brush with hot apricot glaze. Cover with a layer of marzipan then a layer of brown fondant.

3 Mark the lid of the treasure chest with a sharp knife.

4 Lay strips of fondant over the chest to mark the panels.

5 Put the coconut in a bowl and mix in a few drops of green colouring. Spread a little royal icing over the cake board and press the 'grass' lightly into it.

6 Cut out the padlock and handles. Cut a keyhole shape from the padlock and shape the handles over a small box. Leave to dry. Stick on the padlock and handles with royal icing. Paint them gold and stick silver balls on the handles and padlock with royal icing to look like nails. Arrange the chocolate money around the chest

Fairy Castle

Allow plenty of time to cover the cake with royal icing as it is quite a delicate job. If the icing dries too quickly, dip the palette knife into hot water to help smooth the surface.

20cm/8in round cake
115g/4oz/¾ cup butter icing
apricot glaze
675g/1½lb/4½ cups marzipan
8 mini Swiss rolls
675g/1½lb/4½ cups royal icing
food colourings: pink, blue and green
jelly diamonds
4 ice cream cones
2 ice cream wafers
50g/2oz/1 cup desiccated coconut
marshmallows

Equipment
30cm/12in square cake board
wooden cocktail stick (toothpick)

1 Split and fill the cake with butter icing, place in the centre of the board and brush with hot apricot glaze. Cover with a layer of marzipan. Cover the Swiss rolls separately with marzipan. Stick at regular intervals around the cake. Cut the remaining pieces of swiss roll in half.

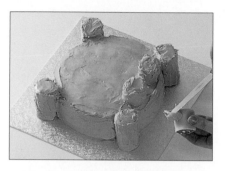

2 Colour two-thirds of the royal icing pale pink and spread evenly over the cake. Cover the extra pieces of Swiss roll in icing and stick round the top of the cake. Using a cocktail stick, score the walls with brick patterns and stick jelly diamonds on the corner towers as windows. Cut the ice cream cones to fit the turrets and stick them in place. Leave to dry overnight.

3 Colour half the remaining royal icing pale blue and spread thinly over the cones, using a fork to pattern the icing.

4 Cut the wafers to shape the gates, stick to the cake and cover with blue icing, marking planks with the back of a knife.

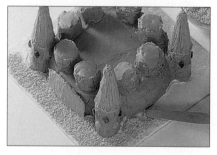

5 Put the coconut in a bowl and mix in a few drops of green colouring. Spread the board with the remaining royal icing and sprinkle over the coconut. Stick the marshmallows on the small turrets with a little royal icing.

COOK'S TIP
When rolling out marzipan, do not sprinkle your work surface with cornstarch because it can dry out the marzipan and cause it to crack.

Treasure Map

Allow several days to paint the map because each colour must dry completely before adding another. Use a fairly dry paint brush to apply the colour.

25cm/10in square cake
225g/8oz/1½ cups butter icing
apricot glaze
450g/1lb/3 cups marzipan
450g/1lb/3 cups white fondant
225g/8oz/1½ cups yellow fondant
food colourings: yellow, brown, paprika,
    green, black and red
115g/4oz/¾ cup royal icing

Equipment
25 x 35cm/10 x 14in cake board
no. 7 shell tube
no. 1 writing tube
soft paint brush

1 Split and fill the cake with butter icing. Cut into a 20 x 25cm/8 x 10in rectangle and place on the board. Brush with apricot glaze. Cover with marzipan then white fondant. Roll out the yellow fondant and cut in a uneven outline.

2 Stick onto the cake with water and dry. Mark out on the map features such as the river. With brown and paprika colours and a paint brush, paint the edges of the map to look old and smudge with kitchen paper. Paint the island green and the water around the island, river and lake blue. Dry before adding other details.

3 Pipe a border of royal icing around the base of the cake with a shell tube. Colour a little royal icing red and pipe the path to the treasure, marked with an 'X'. Colour some icing green and pipe on grass and trees. Colour some icing black and pipe on a North sign with a no. I tube.

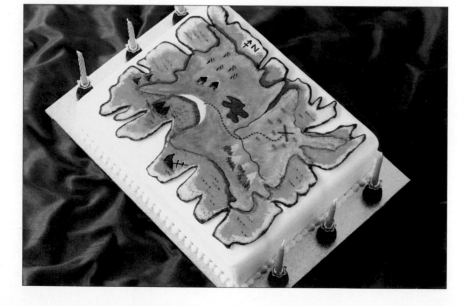

Pirate's Hat

Black fondant may be purchased from specialist cake decorating shops. It is advisable to buy it ready-made rather than attempt to colour it black yourself.

25cm/10in round cake
225g/8oz/1½ cups butter icing
apricot glaze
450g/1lb/3 cups marzipan
450g/1lb/3 cups black fondant
115g/4oz/¾ cup white fondant
food colourings: black and gold
chocolate money
jewel sweets

Equipment
30cm/12in square cake board

1 Split and fill the cake with butter icing. Cut in half and sandwich the halves together. Stand upright diagonally across the cake board and use a template to cut shallow dips to create the crown of the hat. Brush with hot apricot glaze.

2 Cut a strip of marzipan to lay over the top of the cake to neaten the joints. Cover the whole cake with a layer of marzipan then black fondant.

3 Roll out the white fondant, cut 1cm/½in strips and stick in place around the brim of the hat with a little water.

4 Mark the strip with a fork to look like braid. With a template, mark the skull and cross bones; cut out of the white fondant and stick in place with water. Paint the braid strip gold and arrange the chocolate money and jewel sweets on the board.

Royal Crown

The most difficult part of this cake is holding up the covered ice cream wafers while they dry in place. Plenty of royal icing can be used to smooth the joins and help to support the pieces.

20cm/8in round cake
15cm/6in round cake
175g/6oz/scant cup butter icing
apricot glaze
450g/1lb/3 cups marzipan
450g/1lb/3 cups white fondant
115g/4oz/¾ cup red fondant
food colouring: red
450g/1lb/3 cups royal icing
small black jelly sweets (candies)
4 ice cream fan wafers
silver balls
jewel sweets (candies)

Equipment
30cm/12in square cake board
wooden cocktail sticks (toothpicks)

1 Split and fill the cakes with a little butter icing. Sandwich one on top of the other and place on the board. Shape the top cake into a dome. Brush with hot apricot glaze and cover with a layer of marzipan then white fondant.

2 Roll out the red fondant and cover the dome of the cake. Trim away the excess with a knife.

3 Spoon rough mounds of royal icing around the base of the cake and stick a black jelly sweet on each mound.

4 Cut the ice cream wafers in half.

5 Spread both sides of the wafers with royal icing and stick to the cake, smoothing the icing level with the sides of the cake. Use cocktail sticks as support until the icing is dry. Put silver balls on top of each point and jewel sweets around the sides of the crown, sticking in place with a little royal icing.

COOK'S TIP
A silver or gold cake board would be perfect for the royal crown. If you cannot find one, simply cover a plain board with foil.

Frog Prince

Some advance preparation is needed for this cake; the crown should be made first, since it takes around 48 hours to completely dry before being painted.

20cm/8in round cake
115g/4oz/¾ cup butter icing
apricot glaze
45g/1lb/3 cups marzipan
450g/1lb/3 cups green fondant
50g/2oz/¼ cup white fondant
115g/4oz/¾ cup royal icing
food colourings: green, red, black and gold
cornflour (cornstarch) for dusting

Equipment
25cm/10in square cake board

1 Split the cake and fill with butter icing. Cut it in half and sandwich both halves together with apricot glaze. Stand upright diagonally across the cake board.

COOK'S TIP
For more authenticity, you could sit the frog on a bed of desiccated coconut that has been first dyed blue. Use fondant icing dyed a darker green to cut out lily pad shapes.

2 Brush the cake with hot apricot glaze. Cover with a layer of marzipan then green fondant.

3 To make the legs and feet, roll green fondant into 20cm/8in lengths about 1cm/½in in diameter. Fold in half for the back legs and stick on with a little water. The front legs are rolled into 10cm/4in lengths, folded in half and pinched to taper to the foot end. The feet are made in the same way, cut to 4cm/1½in lengths and pinched to tapered ends.

4 Stick in place with a little royal icing. Roll balls for the eyes and stick in place on top of the cake.

5 Roll out the white fondant. Cut a strip 5 x 19cm/2 x 7½in and mark one edge at 2.5cm/1in intervals then cut out triangles to make the crown. Wrap around a glass dusted with cornflour and moisten the edges to join. Leave to dry (up to 2 days). Cut a 10cm/4in circle for the shirt. Stick in place and trim the edge level with the board. Cut white circles and stick to the eyes. Use pink fondant to roll into a rope, stick on for the mouth. Colour a little fondant black, roll and cut pupils for the eyes and bow tie, stick in place.

6 Paint the crown gold and stick into position with royal icing.

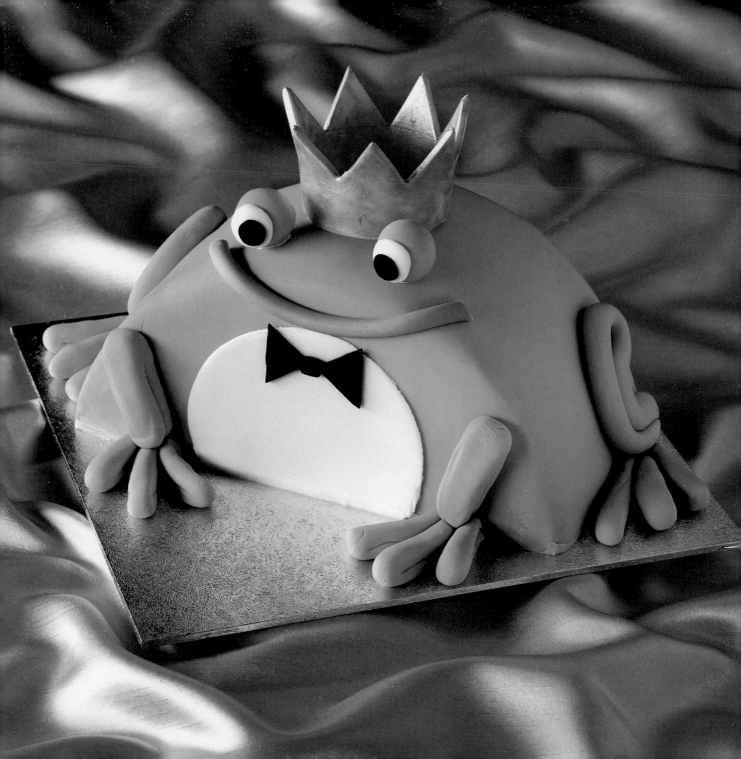

Fairy

This is one of the more advanced cakes and requires a lot of skill and patience. Allow yourself plenty of time if you are attempting the techniques for the first time.

20cm/8in round cake
115g/4oz/¾ cup butter icing
apricot glaze
450g/1lb/3 cups marzipan
400g/14oz/2¾ cups pale blue fondant
50g/2oz/¼ cup white fondant
food colourings: blue, pink, yellow
    and gold
115g/4oz/½ cup royal icing
silver balls

Equipment
25cm/10in cake board
no. 1 piping tube
fine paint brush, no. 2 or 3
twinkle pink sparkle lustre powder
garrett frill cutter
small circle cutter
wooden cocktail stick (toothpick)
cotton wool
no. 7 star tube
silver ribbon

1 Split and fill the cake with butter icing. Place on the board and brush with apricot glaze. Cover with a thin layer of marzipan then pale blue fondant. Leave to dry overnight. Using a template, mark the position of the fairy on the cake. As royal icing dries quickly, work only on about 2.5cm/1in sections of the fairy's wings at a time. Fill a piping bag with a no. I tube with white royal icing and carefully pipe over the outline of each wing section.

2 Pipe a second line just inside that and with a damp paint brush, brush long strokes from the edges toward the centre, leaving more icing at the edges and fading to a thin film near the base of the wings. Dry for I hour. Brush with dry lustre powder (not dissolved in spirit).

3 Colour a little fondant flesh colour, roll and cut out the body. Place in position. Dampen a paint brush, remove excess water on kitchen paper and brush under the arms, legs and head to stick. Round off sharp edges by rubbing gently. Cut out the bodice and shoes and stick in place. Cut out a wand and star and leave to dry.

4 Work quickly to make the tutu, as thin fondant dries quickly and will crack easily. Each frill must be made separately. Roll out a small piece of fondant to 3mm/ ⅛in thick and cut out a fluted circle with a small plain inner circle. (The depth of the frill will be governed by the size of the central hole; the smaller the central hole, the wider the frill.)

5 Cut into quarters and with a wooden cocktail stick, roll along the fluted edge to stretch it and give fullness.

6 Attach the frills to the waist with a little water. Repeat with the other layers, tucking the sides under neatly. Use a wooden cocktail stick to arrange the frills and small pieces of cotton wool to hold the folds of the skirt in place until dry. Leave to dry overnight. Brush a little lustre powder over the edge of the tutu. Paint on the hair and face, stick on the wand and star and paint the star gold. Pipe a border of royal icing round the edge of the board with a star nozzle and place a silver ball on each point. Leave to dry. Colour a little royal icing yellow and pipe over the hair. Paint with a touch of gold colouring.

Pinball Machine

Allow plenty of time to decorate this cake and remember to keep all the different coloured fondants tightly wrapped in separate pieces of clear film to prevent them drying out.

25cm/10in square cake
225g/8oz/1½ cups butter icing
apricot glaze
450g/1lb/3 cups marzipan
115g/4oz/¾ cup royal icing
450g/1lb/3 cups white fondant
food colourings: yellow, blue, green
    and pink
sweets (candies)
2 ice cream fan wafers

Equipment
30cm/12in square cake board
no. 1 writing tube

1 Split the cake and fill with butter icing. Cut off 5cm/2in strip from one side and reserve.

2 Using a sharp serrated knife, cut a thin wedge off the top of the cake, diagonally along its length, to end just above the half way mark. This will give a sloping top.

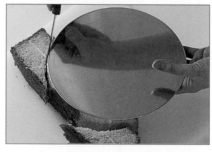

3 Using a 20cm/8in cake tin as a guide, cut an arched back from the reserved cake. Brush cakes with hot apricot glaze. Cover separately with a layer of marzipan and place on the board, sticking together with royal icing. Leave to dry overnight.

4 Cover with a layer of fondant. Leave to dry. Using a template, mark out a design on top of the cake. Colour the fondant in different colours, roll out and cut to fit each section. Stick with water and smooth the joins carefully.

5 Use royal icing to stick sweets on the cake as buffers, flippers, lights and knobs. Roll blue fondant into a long sausage and edge the pinball table and divider. Cut a zig-zag design for the sides and a small screen for the back. Stick on with water. Stick the ice cream fans at the back. Load the pinball sweets. Add the name on the screen with run-out letters or piping.

Camping Tent

The perfect cake for the eager camper. You may find it easier to cover the sides of the cake first, and then the top, rather than all at once.

20cm/8in square cake
115g/4oz/¾ cup butter icing
apricot glaze
450g/1lb/3 cups marzipan
50g/2oz/¼ cup brown fondant
450g/1lb/3 cups orange fondant
food colourings: orange, brown, green, red, yellow and blue
115g/4oz/¾ cup royal icing
50g/2oz/1 cup desiccated coconut
chocolate matchsticks

Equipment
25cm/10in square cake board
wooden cocktail sticks (toothpicks)
fine paint brush
no. 1 plain tube
basket weave tube

2 Stick the two wedges, back to back, on the oblong with apricot glaze to form the tent. Measure the height from the 'ground' and trim off at 10cm/4in high. Use the trimmings on either side of the base. Place the cake diagonally on the board and brush with apricot glaze.

4 Stick halved cocktail sticks in the corners as pegs and in the ridge as poles. Put the coconut in a bowl and mix in a little green colouring. Spread the cake board with a thin layer of royal icing and sprinkle with the coconut.

1 Split and fill the cake with a little butter icing. Cut the cake in half. Cut one half in two diagonally from the top right edge to the bottom left edge to form the roof of the tent.

3 Cover with marzipan. Cover one end of the tent with brown fondant and the rest with orange fondant. Cut and opening for the tent and stick on with water. Cut a 7.5cm/3in slit at the front of the tent, lay over the brown fondant then trim excess. Smooth the joins at the top. Fold back the sides, secure with royal icing. Leave to dry.

5 Colour 50g/2oz/⅓ cup of marzipan flesh coloured, roll a ball for the head, a tiny wedge for the nose and shape the body and arms. Paint a blue T-shirt on to the body and leave to dry. Colour some of the royal icing brown and pipe on the hair with a basket weave tube. Pipe on the mouth and eyes. Make a bonfire with broken chocolate matchsticks.

Sailing Boat

For chocolate lovers, make a chocolate-flavoured sponge by substituting 50g/2oz cocoa for the same quantity of flour. Vary the ornaments according to the child's preferences.

20cm/8in square cake
225g/8oz/1½ cups butter icing
15ml/1tbsp cocoa
4 large chocolate flakes
115g/4oz/¾ cup royal icing
food colouring: blue

Equipment
25cm/10in square cake board
rice paper
round circle cutter
red and blue powder tints
paint brush and plastic drinking straw
wooden cocktail stick (toothpick)
2 small cake ornaments

1 Split and fill the cake with half the butter icing. Cut a 20 x 13cm/8 x 5in rectangle from the cake, then cut it to shape the hull of the boat. Place the hull diagonally across the cake board. Mix the cocoa into the remaining butter icing and spread evenly over the top and sides of the boat. Split the flakes lengthways and press horizontally into the icing to resemble planks of wood.

2 Cut a flake in short lengths for the rudder and tiller and place at the stern. Sprinkle the crumbs over the top.

3 To make the sails, cut a piece of rice paper 14 x 16cm/5½ x 6½in and another piece 15 x 7.5cm/6 x 3in. With sharp scissors, cut the large sail in a gentle curve, starting at the top and working down to the widest part of the paper. Cut the smaller one into a triangle. Using the round cutter to contain the powder tint, brush onto the smooth side of the rice paper, working it in carefully. Remove the cutter.

4 Cut a triangular flag and colour it red. (Do not use liquid colours as they might run.) Wet the edges of the rice paper and stick it onto the straw, holding it in position until it is stuck. Make a hole for the straw 7.5cm/3in from the bow of the boat and push into the cake about 2.5cm/1in with the small sail at the front and the large one at the back.

5 Stick the flag onto a cocktail stick and insert it into the straw. Colour the royal icing blue and spread on the board so that it looks like waves. Place the small ornaments on the boat.

Sand Castle

Crushed digestive biscuits are used to cover this fun cake. It is ideal for children who do not like the richness of butter icing as only a very small amount is used to sandwich the cake.

2 x 15cm/6in round cake
100g/4oz/¾ cup butter icing
apricot glaze
115g/4oz/⅔ cup digestive biscuits
    (graham crackers)
115g/4oz/¾ cup royal icing
food colouring: blue
sweets (candies)

Equipment
25cm/10in square cake board
rice paper
plastic drinking straw
candles

1 Split the cakes and sandwich all the layers together with butter icing. Place on the cake board. Cut 3cm/1¼in off the top just above the filling and shape the rest of the cake so that it has slightly sloping sides.

2 Cut 4 x 3cm/1¼in cubes from the reserved piece and stick on for the turrets. Brush with hot apricot glaze.

3 Crush the digestive biscuits and press through a sieve to make the 'sand'. Press on the crushed biscuits, using a palette knife to get a smooth finish. Colour some royal icing blue and spread around the sand castle on the board to make a moat. Spread a little royal icing around the board and sprinkle on sand. Make a flag with rice paper and half a straw and stick it into the cake. Stick candles into the turrets and arrange the sweets on the board.

Dart Board

Start the decoration several days before the cake is needed, as lots of patience and time is required. If the cake is well sealed to begin with, the decoration can be worked on in stages.

25cm/10in round cake
175g/6oz/scant cup butter icing
apricot glaze
450g/1lb/3 cups marzipan
450g/1lb/3 cups black fondant
115g/4oz/¾ cup yellow fondant
7g/¹⁄₄oz/1 tsp red fondant
115g/4oz/¾ cup royal icing
food colourings: black, yellow, red
    and silver

Equipment
30cm/12in round cake board
1cm/½in plain circle cutter
no. 1 writing tube
candles

1 Split the cake and fill with butter icing. Put onto the board and brush with apricot glaze. Cover with marzipan then black fondant. Wrap the rest in clear film. Use a template to mark the board into sections. Draw a 20cm/8in circle on greaseproof paper, cut out and fold in quarters. Mark each quarter into five portions and draw in lines to meet in the centre. Place the template on the cake; mark the centre and the edge of each wedge on the cake.

2 Mark the wedges on the top of the cake with a sharp knife. Roll out the yellow fondant and cut out wedges, using the template as a guide. Place on alternate sections but do not stick in place yet. Repeat with the rest of the black fondant.

3 Carefully cut 3mm/¹⁄₈in off each wedge and swop the colours. Mark a 13cm/5in circle in the centre of the board and cut out 3mm/¹⁄₈in pieces to swap with adjoining colours. Stick in place and use an icing smoother to flatten.

4 Use the cutter to remove the centre for the bull's eye. Cut out and stick on a red fondant bull's eye and surround with a thin strip of black fondant. Roll the remaining black fondant into a long sausage to fit round the base of the cake and stick in place with a little water.

5 Mark numbers onto the board and pipe on with royal icing using a no. I tube. Leave to dry then paint the numbers with silver. Stick candles into the cake at an angle to resemble darts.

Flight Simulation Game

This is a small cake to give to a video-game enthusiast. The fine rope is made by rolling the fondant on a smooth surface with a perspex smoother to give a neat continuous finish.

15cm/6in square cake
115g/4oz/¾ cup butter icing
apricot glaze
225g/8oz/1½ cups marzipan
225g/8oz/1½ cups black fondant
50g/2oz/¼ cup white fondant
food colourings: black, blue, red
　　and yellow
royal icing

Equipment
20cm/8in square cake board
wooden cocktail stick (toothpick)
fine paint brush

1 Split and fill the cake with butter icing. With a sharp serrated knife, cut 2.5cm/1in off one side of the cake and 1cm/½in off the other. Round the corners. Place on the board and brush with apricot glaze.

2 Cover with marzipan then black fondant. With a cocktail stick mark the speaker holes and position of screen and knobs. Colour half the white fondant pale blue, roll out and cut a 6cm/2½in square for the screen. Stick in the centre of the computer with water. Colour a small piece red and the rest yellow. Cut out a start switch 2.5cm/1in long from red, and controls from yellow. Stick down with water. Roll remaining black fondant into a thin sausage to edge the screen and base of the cake.

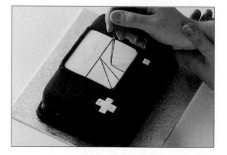

3 With a paint brush, draw the game onto the screen with blue colour. Pipe letters onto the buttons with a little royal icing.

Sheet of Music

This cake is ideal for young musicians. As it requires very delicate piping, it is advisable to practise first before attempting to decorate this cake.

25cm/10in square cake
225g/8oz/1½ cups butter icing
apricot glaze
450g/1lb/3 cups marzipan
450g/1lb/3 cups white fondant
115g/4oz/¾ cup royal icing
food colouring: black

Equipment
25 x 30cm/10 x 12in
   cake board
no. 0 writing tube
no. 7 shell tube
1.30m/1½ yards ribbon

1 Split the cake and fill with butter icing. Cut 5cm/2in off one side of the cake so that it measures 20 x 25cm/8 x 10in.

2 Place on the cake board and brush with hot apricot glaze. Cover with a layer of marzipan then white fondant. Leave to dry overnight. With a template, mark out the sheet of music and child's name.

3 Pipe the lines and bars first with white royal icing and a no. 0 tube then colour the remaining icing black and pipe the clefs, name and notes. Pipe a royal icing border around the base of the cake with the shell tube and tie a ribbon around the cake.

Doll's House

Little children will love this cake, especially if you pipe their age on the door. The same number of candles can be added to the cake if you wish.

25cm/10in square cake
225g/8oz/1½ cups butter icing
apricot glaze
450g/1lb/3 cups marzipan
450g/1lb/3 cups white fondant
food colourings: red, yellow, blue, black,
    green and gold
115g/4oz/¾ cup royal icing

Equipment
30cm/12in square cake board
no. 2 writing tube
flower decorations

1 Split and fill the cake with butter icing. Cut 6cm/2½in triangles off two corners then use these pieces to make a chimney. Place on the cake board and brush with hot apricot glaze. Cover with a layer of marzipan then white fondant.

COOK'S TIP
Always keep icing covered when not in use, to prevent it drying out.

2 Using a pastry wheel, mark the roof to look like thatch. Mark the chimney with the back of a knife to look like bricks.

3 Paint the chimney with red food colouring and the roof with yellow.

4 Mark the door 7.5 x 12cm/3 x 4½in and the windows 6cm/2½in square. Colour 25g/1oz/2 tbsp of fondant red, cut out and stick on the door with water. Colour a piece blue, cut out and stick on for the fanlight. Paint the curtains with blue food colour. Colour half the royal icing black and pipe the window frames and panes, around the door and fanlight.

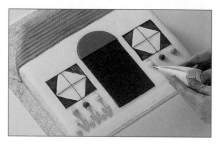

5 Colour the remaining royal icing green. Pipe flowers under the windows and the climber up the wall and onto the roof. Stick in place with icing and pipe green flower centres. Pipe the age of the child on the door. Dry for 1 hour. Paint the knocker, handle and number in gold.

Circus

This design is very easy to achieve. The miniature circus ornaments measure 5cm/2in high and can be bought from party shops, although anything similar can be used.

20cm/8in round cake
115g/4oz/¾ cup butter icing
apricot glaze
450g/1lb/3 cups marzipan
450g/1lb/3 cups white fondant
food colourings: red and blue
115g/4oz/¾ cup royal icing
3 digestive biscuits (graham crackers)
silver balls

Equipment
25cm/10in round cake board
no. 5 star tube
small plastic circus ornaments

1 Split the cake and fill with a little butter icing. Place on the cake board and brush with apricot glaze.

2 Cover with marzipan then white fondant. Colour 115g/4oz/¾ cup of fondant pink, roll into a rope and stick around the top edge of the cake to make a wall. Colour half the remaining fondant red and the other half blue. Roll out each and cut into twelve 2.5cm/1in squares. Stick alternately at an angle around the side of the cake with water. Pipe stars around the base of the cake with royal icing and stick in silver balls as you work.

3 Crush the digestive biscuits by pressing through a sieve to make the 'sand'. Scatter over the top of the cake and place small circus ornaments on top.

Drum

This is a colourful cake for very young children. The ropes can be made by rolling by hand on a smooth work surface, but a perspex smoother will give a better result.

15cm/6in round cake
50g/2oz/¼ cup butter icing
apricot glaze
350g/12oz/2¼ cups marzipan
450g/1lb/3 cups white fondant
food colourings: red, blue and yellow

Equipment
20cm/8in round cake board

1 Split and fill the cake with a little butter icing. Place on the cake board and brush with hot apricot glaze. Cover with a layer of marzipan and leave to dry overnight. Colour half the fondant red. Roll out to 25 x 30cm/10 x 12in and cut in half. Stick to the sides of the cake with water, smoothing the joins neatly.

2 Roll out a circle of white fondant to fit the top of the cake and divide the rest in half. Colour one half blue and the other yellow. Divide the blue into four equal pieces and roll each piece into a sausage long enough to go half way round the cake. Stick around the base and top of the cake with a little water.

3 To denote the position of the ropes, mark the cake into six around the top and bottom using greaseproof paper marked in six wedges.

4 Roll the yellow fondant into strands to cross diagonally on the side. Roll the rest of the yellow fondant into 12 balls and stick at each end of the strings. Knead red and white fondant together until streaky and roll two balls and sticks 15cm/6in long. Dry. Stick to drum with royal icing.

Clown Face

Children of all ages will love this smiling clown. His frilly collar is quite easy to make, but you do need to work quickly before the fondant dries.

20cm/8in round cake
115g/4oz/¾ cup butter icing
apricot glaze
450g/1lb/3 cups marzipan
450g/1lb/3 cups white fondant
115g/4oz/¾ cup royal icing
food colourings: pink, red, green, blue and black
silver balls

Equipment
25cm/10in round cake board
no. 8 star tube
garrett frill cutter
small circle cutter
wooden cocktail stick (toothpick)
cotton wool
candles

1 Split and fill the cake with butter icing. Place in the centre of the cake board and brush with hot apricot glaze. Cover with a thin layer of marzipan then white fondant. Mark the position of the features. Pipe stars around the base of the cake with royal icing, placing silver balls as you work, and leave to dry overnight.

2 Colour half the remaining fondant pale pink, roll out and with the use of a template, cut out the shape of the face. Lay on the cake with the top of the head touching one edge of the cake.

3 Colour the remaining pink fondant red, roll out and cut out the nose. Roll out some of the white fondant, cut out the eyes and mouth and stick on the face with the nose, using a little water. Roll out a little of the red fondant into a thin sausage and cut to fit the mouth. Stick in place with a little water.

4 Roll out the rest of the red fondant, cut in strands for hair and stick with water.

5 Colour most of the remaining fondant pale green and roll out thinly. Cut out a fluted circle with a small plain inner circle. Cut through one side and roll along the fluted edge with a cocktail stick to stretch it. Stick on the cake with a little water and arrange the frills. Repeat to make three layers of frills, holding them in place with cotton wool until dry.

6 Colour a little fondant blue, roll and cut out eyes and stick in place with a little water. Colour the rest of the fondant black, roll and cut out the eyes and eyebrows, then stick in position. Place the candles at the top of the head.

Kite

The happy face on this cheerful kite uses the same template pattern as the Clown Face cake, and is a great favourite with children of all ages.

25cm/10in square cake
225g/8oz/1½ cups butter icing
apricot glaze
450g/1lb/3 cups marzipan
450g/1lb/3 cups pale yellow fondant
225g/8oz/1½ cups white fondant
115g/4oz/¾ cup royal icing
food colourings: yellow, red, green, blue
    and black

Equipment
30cm/12in square cake board
no. 8 star tube
candles

1 Split and fill the cake with butter icing. Mark 15cm/6in from one corner down two sides and using a ruler from this point cut down to the opposite corner on both sides to get the kite shape. Place diagonally on the cake board and brush with apricot glaze.

COOK'S TIP
If you don't have apricot jam, you can use marmalade instead. Just melt it, strain it then cool before use.

2 Cover with a layer of marzipan then pale yellow fondant. Using a template, mark the face on the kite. Divide the white fondant into four and colour them red, green, blue and black. Wrap each separately in clear film. Pipe a border of shells around the base of the cake.

3 Using a template, cut out the face, bow tie and buttons and stick in place with a little water.

4 To make the kite's tail, roll out each colour separately and cut two 4 x Icm/1½ x ½in lengths from the blue, red and green fondants. Pinch them to shape into bows.

5 Roll the yellow into a long rope and lay it on the board in a wavy line from the narrow end of the kite and stick the bows in place with water. Roll balls of yellow fondant, stick on the board with a little royal icing and press in the candles.

Balloons

This is a simple yet effective design that can be adapted to any age. It will particularly appeal to young children, and it is easy to make and decorate.

20cm/8in round cake
115g/4oz/¾ cup butter icing
apricot glaze
450g/1lb/3 cups marzipan
450g/1lb/3 cups white fondant
food colourings: pink, blue, green and
   yellow
100g/4oz/¾ cup royal icing

Equipment
25cm/10in cake board
1.5m/1¾ yards 4cm/½in wide ribbon
no. 2 plain tube
no. 7 star tube
candles

1 Split and fill the cake with butter icing. Place on the cake board and brush with apricot glaze. Cover with a layer of marzipan then white fondant. Divide the remaining fondant into three pieces; colour one pink, one blue and the other green. Roll out and, using a template, cut out a balloon from each colour. Stick onto the cake with a little water, rubbing the edges gently with a finger to round off any straight edges.

2 Tie the ribbon round the cake. With yellow royal icing and a plain tube, pipe on the strings, attaching them to the balloons. Pipe a border around the base of the cake.

3 Using a pin, prick out a number onto each balloon, then pipe the outline. Arrange the candles on the cake.

Paddling Pool

This fun cake will need a day's preparation; the bather, boat and duck are modelled from marzipan and fondant and dried overnight before arranging them in partly-dried royal icing.

15cm/6in round cake
50g/2oz/¼ cup butter icing
apricot glaze
350g/12oz/2¼ cups marzipan
450g/1lb/3 cups white fondant
food colourings: blue, red, yellow, green
  and brown
115g/4oz/¾ cup royal icing

Equipment
20cm/8in round cake board
no. 1 plain tube
basket weave tube

2 Colour 50g/2oz/⅓ cup of marzipan flesh colour and shape into a small child with a head, half a body, arms and feet. Place into the rubber ring and leave to dry overnight.

3 Colour two-thirds of the royal icing blue and spread on the cake to resemble water. Put the child, duck and boat in the water. Use brown royal icing with a basket weave pipe for the hair. Pipe eyes and mouth.

1 Split the cake and fill with butter icing. Place on the cake board and brush with apricot glaze. Cover with marzipan then white fondant. Divide the rest of the fondant into four pieces and colour them blue, red, yellow and green. Shape a duck from the yellow, a 4-cm/1½-in rubber ring from the red and a boat from the green. Roll the remains of each into two sausages long enough to go half way round the cake. Stick around the cake with water; flatten a little and smooth the joins so the stripes come to the top of the cake.

Chess Board

For this cake to look most effective, the squares should have very sharp edges, so take care to neaten them as you stick them into position.

25cm/10in square cake
225g/8oz/1½ cups butter icing
apricot glaze
800g/1¾lb/5¾ cups marzipan
450g/1lb/3 cups white fondant
food colourings: black and red
silver balls
115g/4oz/¾ cup black fondant
115g/4oz/¾ cup royal icing

Equipment
30cm/12in square cake board
no. 8 star tube

1 Split the cake and fill with butter icing. Place on the cake board and brush with apricot glaze. Roll out 450g/1lb/3 cups of marzipan and cover the cake with a layer of marzipan then white fondant. Leave to dry overnight.

COOK'S TIP
Wear rubber gloves when colouring marzipan with food colouring paste to avoid staining the hands. Knead the marzipan until the colour is evenly distributed throughout.

2 Colour one half of the remaining marzipan black and the other half red. To shape the chess pieces, roll 50g/2oz/¼ cup of marzipan into a sausage and cut into 8 equal pieces then shape into pawns. Divide 75g/3oz/⅔ cup of marzipan into 6 equal pieces then shape into two castles, two knights and two bishops. Divide 25g/1oz/2 tbsp of marzipan in half and shape a queen and a king. Decorate with silver balls. Leave to dry.

3 Mark the cake into eight 3cm/1¼in squares along each side, leaving a border around the edge. Divide the board into 64 equal squares using a sharp knife.

4 Roll out the black fondant and cut into 3cm/1¼in squares. Stick onto alternate squares on the board with a little water, starting with a black square in the bottom left hand corner and finishing with another black square in the top right hand corner.

5 Cut 1cm/½in black strips to edge the board and stick in place with a little water. Pipe a border round the base of the cake with royal icing. Place the chess pieces in position.

Jack-in-the-Box

Instead of making your own numbers, you can use tiny edible flowers or letters and stick them onto the sides of the box.

15cm/6in square cake
50g/2oz/¼ cup butter icing
apricot glaze
350g/12oz/2¼ cups marzipan
450g/1lb/3 cups white fondant
ice cream cone
115g/4oz/¾ cup royal icing
food colourings: blue, black, green, red
    and yellow
silver balls

Equipment
20cm/8in round cake board
garrett frill cutter and plain circle cutter
wooden cocktail stick (toothpick)
cotton wool and no. 8 star tube

1 Split the cake and fill with butter icing. Cut a 5cm/2in rectangle from two sides of the cake to create a 10cm/4in square, a 5cm/2in square and two rectangles. Sandwich the rectangles together on top of the large square. Brush with apricot glaze. Cover with marzipan then white fondant. Shape the last cube of cake into a ball for the head. Brush with glaze, cover with marzipan then white fondant. Dry.

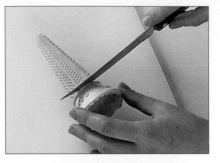

2 Cut the top off the ice cream cone. Stick the wide part of the cone in the centre of the cake with a little royal icing then stick the head on top.

3 Colour a small piece of fondant blue, roll out and cut a fluted circle with a small inner circle. (The depth of the frill will depend on the size of the central hole; the smaller the centre, the wider the frill.) Cut one side and open out then roll the fluted edge with a wooden cocktail stick to stretch it. Attach it to the neck with royal icing; arrange the folds with a cocktail stick and support with cotton wool while they dry. Make a second frill.

4 Stick the ice cream cone hat on the head with a little royal icing. Cut eyes from blue fondant and stick on with water. Colour pieces of fondant black, green and red and roll out. Cut and stick on black eyes. Cut a semi-circle of green, stick around the back of the head and snip with sharp scissors to give spiky hair (or cut two short lengths). Cut out red nose, mouth and numbers for the sides of the box. Stick on with a little water.

5 Colour the remaining royal icing yellow and pipe stars round the edges of the cube and pompoms on the hat, sticking in silver balls as you go.

Toy Car

This little car can be made for any age. You could add a personalized number plate with the child's name and age to the back of the car.

20cm/8in round cake
115g/4oz/¾ cup butter icing
apricot glaze
450g/1lb/3 cups marzipan
450g/1lb/3 cups yellow fondant
50g/2oz/¼ cup red fondant
food colourings: yellow, red and black
30ml/2tbsp royal icing
sweets (candies)

Equipment
25cm/10in round cake board
no. 1 writing tube
candles

1 Split the cake and fill with a little butter icing. Cut in half and sandwich the halves upright together. With a sharp serrated knife, cut a shallow dip to create the wind-screen and to shape the bonnet. Place on the cake board and brush with apricot glaze.

2 Cut a strip of marzipan to cover the top of the cake to level the joins. Then cover with a layer of marzipan then yellow fondant. Leave to dry overnight.

3 Mark the doors and windows onto the car with a sharp skewer.

4 Roll out the red fondant and cut out four 4cm/1½in wheels with a cutter. Stick in place with a little water. Mark the centre of each wheel with a smaller cutter. Colour the royal icing black and pipe over the doors and windows. Stick on sweets for headlights with a little royal icing. Press the candles into sweets and stick to the board with a little royal icing.

Racing Track

This cake will delight all eight-year-old racing car enthusiasts. It's relatively simple to make and can be decorated with as many cars as you like.

2 x 15cm/6in round cake
115g/4oz/¾ cup butter icing
apricot glaze
450g/1lb/3 cups marzipan
450g/1lb/3 cups pale blue fondant
50g/2oz/¼ cup white fondant
food colourings: blue and red
115g/4oz/¾ cup royal icing

Equipment
25 x 35cm/10 x 14in cake board
5cm/2in fluted cutter
no. 8 star tube
no. 2 plain tube
candles
2 small racing cars

1 Split the cakes and fill with a little butter icing. Cut off a lcm/½in piece from one side of each cake and place the cakes on the cake board with the flat edges together. Brush with apricot glaze. Cover with marzipan then pale blue fondant.

2 Mark a 5cm/2in circle in the centre of each cake. Roll out the white fondant, cut out two fluted circles and stick in the marked spaces.

3 Colour the royal icing red. Pipe a shell border around the base of the cake using a no. 8 star tube. Pipe a track for the cars on the cake using a no. 2 plain tube and place the candles on the two white circles. Place the cars on the track.

COOK'S TIP
Vary the colours of the fondant icing and the candles according to the child's favourite shades.

Fire Engine

This jolly fire engine is simplicity itself as the decorations are mainly bought sweets and novelties. It is easier to buy the red fondant ready-coloured, so the cake is quick to prepare.

20cm/8in square cake
115g/4oz/¾ cup butter icing
apricot glaze
350g/12oz/2¼ cups marzipan
350g/12oz/2¼ cups red fondant
liquorice strips
115g/4oz/¾ cup royal icing
food colourings: black and green
115g/4oz/¾ cup white fondant
sweets (candies)
2 silver bells
50g/2oz/1 cup desiccated coconut

Equipment
25cm/10in round cake board
no. 2 plain tube
candles

1 Split and fill the cake with a little butter icing. Cut in half and sandwich one half on top of the other. Place on the cake board and brush with hot apricot glaze.

2 Trim a thin wedge off the front edge to make a sloping windscreen. Cover with a layer of marzipan and red fondant.

3 Mark the windows, ladder and wheels.

4 To make the ladder, cut the liquorice into two strips and short pieces for the rungs. Colour half the royal icing black and stick the ladder to the top of the cake with royal icing. Roll out the white fondant, cut out and stick on the windows with a little water.

5 Pipe round the windows in black royal icing. Stick sweets in place for headlights, lamps and wheels and stick the bells on the roof. Put the coconut in a bowl and mix in a few drops of green colouring. Spread royal icing over the cake board and sprinkle with coconut. Stick sweets to the board with royal icing and add the candles.

Army Tank

Create an authentic-looking camouflaged tank for an army enthusiast by combining green and brown fondant, and a chocolate flake for a gun.

25cm/10in square cake
225g/8oz/1½ cups butter icing
apricot glaze
450g/1lb/3 cups marzipan
350g/12oz/2¼ cups green fondant
115g/4oz/¾ cup brown fondant
food colourings: green and brown
chocolate flake
60ml/4tbsp royal icing
round biscuits (cookies)
sweets (candies)
liquorice strips

Equipment
25 x 35cm/10 x 14in cake board

1 Split the cake and fill with butter icing. Cut off a 15cm/6in rectangle from one side of the cake. Cut a smaller rectangle 15 x 7.5cm/6 x 3in and stick on the top.

2 Using a sharp serrated knife, shape the sloping top and cut a 2.5cm/1in piece from both ends between the tracks. Shape the rounded ends for the wheels and track. Assemble the cake on the cake board and brush with apricot glaze. Cover with marzipan. Roll out the green fondant to about a 25cm/10in square. Break small pieces of brown fondant and place all over the green. Flatten and roll out together to give a camouflage effect.

3 Turn over, brush off excess icing sugar and repeat on the underside. Roll out until the fondant is about 3mm/⅛in thick. Lay the fondant over the cake, gently pressing over the turret and down the sides of the track on both sides. Carefully mould over the tracks, cutting away the excess. Cut a piece into a 6cm/2½in disc and stick on with a little water for the hatch on top. Cut a small hole for the gun and stick the chocolate flake in. Stick liquorice for the tracks, using a little black royal icing. Add on biscuits for the wheels and sweets for the lights and port holes.

Number 6 Cake

Before assembling the cake, use the round tin as a guide to enable you to cut the square cake, so that it will fit neatly around the circular cake.

15cm/6in round cake
15cm/6in square cake
115g/4oz/¾ cup butter icing
apricot glaze
450g/1lb/3 cups marzipan
450g/1lb/3 cups pale yellow fondant
50g/2oz/¼ cup pale green fondant
food colourings: yellow and green
115g/4oz/¾ cup royal icing

Equipment
25 x 35cm/10 x 14in cake board
no. 1 plain tube
no. 8 star tube
7.5cm/3in fluted cutter
plastic train set with 6 candles

1 Split the cakes and fill with a little butter icing. Cut the square cake in half and cut a rounded end from one oblong to fit neatly around the round cake. Trim the cakes to the same depth and assemble on the cake board as shown, and brush with hot apricot glaze. Cover with a thin layer of marzipan. Smooth any joins and make sure the surface is flat.

2 Cover the cake with yellow fondant. Mark a 7.5cm/3in circle in the centre of the round cake. Colour a piece of fondant pale green, roll out and cut out a fluted circle. Stick on with water and dry. Mark the track 2cm/¾in wide or width of the train. Colour royal icing yellow and pipe track with a no. I tube. Using a no. 8 star tube, pipe a border around base and top of the cake. Pipe the name on the green circle and attach the train with royal icing.

Space Ship

For this cake, the triangles for the jets should be covered separately, then stuck into position after decorating. For a more dramatic space ship, use black icing, and vary the other colours.

25cm/10in square cake
225g/8oz/1½ cups butter icing
apricot glaze
350g/12oz/2¼ cups marzipan
450g/1lb/3 cups white fondant
food colourings: blue, pink and black

Equipment
30cm/12in square cake board
candles
gold paper stars

1 Split and fill the cake with a little butter icing. With a sharp serrated knife, cut a 10cm/4in piece diagonally across the middle of the cake and about 25cm/10in long.

2 Shape the nose and cut the remaining cake in three 7.5cm/3in triangles for the sides and top of the ship. Cut two smaller triangles for the boosters and fit any remaining cake down the middle of the space ship. Assemble diagonally across the cake board and brush with apricot glaze. Cover with marzipan then white fondant.

3 Colour one-third of the remaining fondant blue, one-third pink and one-third black. Wrap each in clear film. Roll out the blue and cut in 1cm/½in strips. Stick in a line around the base of the cake and outline the triangles. Stick a 2.5cm/1in strip down the centre of the space ship.

4 Roll out the pink fondant and cut out shapes to decorate the ship. Roll out the black fondant and cut out windows, circles, name and numbers. Stick in place with a little water.

5 With any leftover fondant, make candle holders by shaping into small cubes. Stick the candles into them then stick onto the board. Decorate the board with gold stars.

COOK'S TIP
Unless stated, use a little water to stick trimmings or shapes onto cakes.

Ballerina

This cake requires patience and plenty of time for the decoration. The tiny flowers were made with 5mm/¼in and 9mm/⅜in flower cutters with ejectors.

20cm/8in round cake
115g/4oz/¾ cup butter icing
apricot glaze
450g/1lb/3 cups marzipan
450g/1lb/3 cups white fondant
food colourings: pink, yellow and green
115g/4oz/¾ cup royal icing

Equipment
25cm/10in round cake board
small flower cutter, garrett frill cutter and
    small circle cutter
wooden cocktail stick (toothpick)
cotton wool
fine paint brush
no. 7 shell tube
1.5m/1¾ yards ribbon

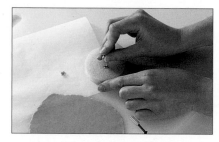

1 Split and fill the cake with butter icing. Place on the board and brush with apricot glaze. Cover with marzipan then white fondant. Dry overnight. Divide remaining fondant into three; colour one flesh tones and the other two in contrasting pinks for the tutu and flowers. Roll out each colour separately and cut out 6 flowers and 3 tiny flowers from the paler pink fondant for the headdress. Leave aside to dry.

2 Using the template, carefully mark the position of the ballerina onto the cake. Cut out the body from flesh coloured fondant and stick into position with a little water. Round off edges by rubbing gently with a finger. Cut out a bodice from the darker pink fondant and stick in place.

3 To make the tutu, work quickly as the thin fondant dries quickly and will crack. Roll out the darker pink fondant to 3mm/⅛in thick and cut out a fluted circle with a small plain inner circle.

4 Cut the circle into quarters and with a wooden cocktail stick, roll along the fluted edge to stretch it and give fullness.

5 Attach the frills to the waist with a little water. Repeat with two more layers, using a cocktail stick to shape the frills and cotton wool to hold them in place until dry. For the final layer, use the paler pink and cover with a short dark frill, as the bodice extension. Leave to dry overnight.

6 Attach flowers to the hoop. Colour royal icing green and pipe leaves in between. Paint on the face and hair. Stick three flowers in place on the head. Cut pale pink shoes and stick in place with water, and paint ribbons. Colour royal icing dark pink and pipe flower centres on the hoop and headdress. Pipe white royal icing around the base of the cake with the shell tube and tie round the ribbon.

Toy Telephone

This is a small retro-style toy cake for children; the numbers on the dial can represent their age. The child's name can be piped in a contrasting colour.

15cm/6in square cake
50g/2oz/¼ cup butter icing
apricot glaze
275g/10oz/2 cups marzipan
350g/12oz/2¼ cups white fondant
food colourings: yellow, blue, red
    and black
liquorice strips
115g/4oz/¾ cup royal icing

Equipment
20cm/8in square cake board
no. 1 writing tube

1 Split the cake and fill with butter icing. Using a sharp knife and a template, cut out the shape of the telephone. Round off the edges and cut a shallow groove where the handle rests on the telephone. Place on the cake board and brush with apricot glaze.

2 Cover the cake with marzipan then white fondant. Colour half the remaining fondant yellow, roll out and cut a 7.5cm/3in circle for the dial. Colour a small piece blue and the rest of the fondant red and cut out 12 small red discs for the numbers (with a piping tube) and a 5cm/2in blue disc for the centre. Stick into place with a little water.

3 Twist the liquorice around to curl it for the cord, stick the ends to the fondant and secure with royal icing. Colour the royal icing black and pipe numbers and the name of child on the telephone.

Box of Chocolates

This sophisticated cake is perfect for a very grown-up birthday and will delight chocolate lovers young and old. Substitute 40g/1½oz flour for cocoa to make a chocolate sponge.

15cm/6in square cake
50g/2oz/¼ cup butter icing
apricot glaze
350g/12oz/2¼ cups marzipan
225g/8oz/1½ cups red fondant
115g/4oz/¾ cup white fondant
food colouring: red
chocolates

Equipment
20cm/8in square cake board
small paper sweet (candy) cases
1.30m/1½ yards 4cm/1½in-wide gold
    and red ribbon

1 Split the cake and fill with a little butter icing. With a sharp knife, cut a shallow square from the top of the cake, leaving a Icm/½in border around the edge. Place on the cake board and brush with apricot glaze. Cover with a layer of marzipan.

COOK'S TIP
It looks smart to match the colour of the fondant to the chocolates that have been selected.

2 Roll out the white fondant and cut into an 18cm/7in square. Lay it in the hollow dip and trim off the excess. Roll out the red fondant and cover the sides.

3 Put the chocolates into coloured paper cases and arrange in the box. Wrap the ribbon around the sides and tie in a large bow.

Rosette Cake

Although it may look intricate, this cake is actually very quick to decorate. If the icing becomes too soft, put it in the fridge. If you make a mistake, you can try again to get a good finish.

20cm/8in square cake
350g/12oz/2¼ cups butter icing
apricot glaze
food colouring: mulberry red
crystallized violets

Equipment
25cm/10in square cake board
cake comb
no. 8 star tube
candles

2 Colour the remaining butter icing dark pink. Spread the top and sides with butter icing. Using the cake comb; hold it against the cake and move it from side to side across the top to make waves. Hold the comb against the side of the cake, resting the flat edge on the board, draw along to give straight ridges down each side.

1 Split the cake and fill with butter icing. Place on the cake board and brush with apricot glaze.

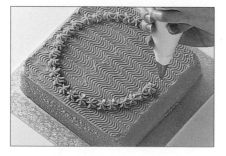

3 Put the rest of the butter icing into a piping bag fitted with a star tube. Mark a 15cm/6in circle on the top of the cake and pipe stars around it and around the base of the cake. Place the candles and flowers in the corners.

Gift-wrapped Parcel

If you do not have a tiny flower cutter for the design on the 'wrapping paper' then press a small decorative button into the fondant while still soft to create a pattern.

15cm/6in square cake
50g/2oz/¼ cup butter icing
apricot glaze
450g/1lb/3 cups marzipan
350g/12oz/2¼ cups pale lemon fondant
food colourings: yellow, red and green
30ml/2 tbsp royal icing

Equipment
20cm/8in square cake board
small flower cutter (optional)

1 Split the cake and fill with butter icing. Place on a board and brush with apricot glaze. Cover with half the marzipan then yellow fondant and mark with a small cutter. Divide the remaining marzipan in half, colour one half pink and the other green. Roll out the pink marzipan and cut into four 2.5 x 18cm /1 x 7in strips. Roll out the green marzipan and cut into four 1cm/½in strips the same length.

2 Centre the green strips on the pink strips and stick on to the cake with water. Cut two 5 cm/2in strips from each colour and cut a V to form the ends of the ribbon. Stick in place and dry overnight.

3 Cut the rest of the green into 2.5 x 7.5cm/1 x 3in lengths and the pink into 1 x 7.5cm/½ x 3in lengths. Centre the pink on top of the green, fold in half, stick ends together and slip over the handle of a wooden spoon, dusted with cornflour.

4 Leave to dry overnight. Cut the ends in V shapes to fit neatly together on the cake. Cut a piece for the join in the centre, and fold in half with the join at the bottom. Remove the bows from the spoon and stick in position with royal icing.

Twisted Ribbon Cake

This cake would be ideal for a celebration such as a christening or the birth of a new baby. Allow a couple of days to decorate the cake.

20cm/8in round cake
115g/4oz/¾ cup butter icing
apricot glaze
450g/1lb/3 cups marzipan
450g/1lb/3 cups pale yellow fondant
115g/4oz/¾ cup white fondant
115g/4oz/¾ cup royal icing
food colourings: yellow and blue
pink dusting powder

Equipment
25cm/10in round cake board
no. 1 piping tube
6 small blue bows

1 Split and fill the cake with butter icing. Place on the board and brush with hot apricot glaze. Cover with a thin layer of marzipan then pale yellow fondant, extending it over the board. Measure the circumference of the cake with a piece of string and cut a strip of paper of the same length and depth as the cake. Fold the paper into six sections, mark with a deep scallop and cut in the top edge. Use to mark the swags on the side of the cake with a sharp needle.

2 Colour 40g/½oz/1 tbsp of white fondant pale blue and roll out thinly. Wet a paint brush with water, remove excess on kitchen paper and brush lightly over the fondant. Roll out thinly the same quantity of white fondant, lay this on top and press together. Roll out together to a 20cm/8in square.

3 Cut 5mm/¼in strips, carefully twist each one, moisten the swag marks with water and drape each barley twist into place, pressing lightly to stick to the cake.

4 Using a template, mark the knitting in the centre of the cake. Cut out the jersey from white fondant and stick down. Roll a little fondant into a ball and colour a small amount blue. Roll into two tapering 7.5cm/3in long needles with a small ball for the end. Dry overnight.

5 Stick needles and ball in position and with royal icing and a no. I tube, pipe knitting and stitches over needles and a trail of wool to the ball. Pipe over the ball with wool. Pipe a border around the base of the cake. Stick on bows around the edge and brush knitting with powder tints.

Sweethearts

The heart-shaped run-outs can be made a week before the cake is made to ensure that they are completely dry. Once these are made, the cake can be quickly decorated.

20cm/8in round cake
115g/4oz/¾ cup butter icing
apricot glaze
450g/1lb/3 cups marzipan
675g/1½lb/4½ cups pink fondant
food colouring: red
115g/4oz/¾ cup royal icing

Equipment
25cm/10in round cake board
no. 1 writing tube
1.5m/1¾ yards 2.5cm/1in ribbon
candles

2 Using a template, make the heart-shaped run-outs. Leave to dry for at least 48 hours.

3 Arrange the hearts on top of the cake and place the candles in the centre. Tie the ribbon around the cake.

1 Split and fill the cake with butter icing. Place on the cake board and brush with apricot glaze. Cover with a layer of marzipan then a layer of pink fondant, large enough to cover the cake and the board. Smooth the surface and trim off the excess. Mark the edge with the decorative handle of a spoon.

Number 10 Cake

This is a very simple cake and it is easy to decorate. If you find the shell edge difficult to pipe, then simply pipe stars around the edges to neaten.

20cm/8in round cake
15cm/6in round cake
450g/1lb/3 cups butter icing
apricot glaze
sugar strands
food colouring: red

Equipment
25cm/10in round cake board
wooden cocktail stick (toothpick)
plastic number 10 cake decoration
no. 7 shell tube
no. 7 star tube
candles

1 Split both cakes and fill with a little butter icing. Brush the sides with apricot glaze. When cold, spread a layer of butter icing on the sides then roll in sugar strands to cover.

COOK'S TIP
Chocolate vermicelli can be used in place of the sugar strands to cover the sides of the cakes.

2 Colour the rest of the icing pink, spread over the top of each cake. Place the small cake on top of the large cake. Using a cocktail stick, make a pattern in the icing on top of the cake.

3 Use the remaining pink icing to pipe around the base and edge of the cakes. Stick the number 10 decoration on the top tier with two candles. Arrange the other candles around the bottom cake.

Cloth Cake

This cake is so named because it looks rather like a white lacy cloth draped over a red tablecloth. It would be perfect for an older child.

20cm/8in round cake
115g/4oz/¾ cup butter icing
apricot glaze
450g/1lb/3 cups marzipan
450g/1lb/3 cups red fondant
225g/8oz/1½ cups white fondant
115g/4oz/¾ cup royal icing
food colouring: red

Equipment
25cm/10in round cake board
no. 1 piping tube
no. 0 plain tube
no. 2 plain tube
wooden cocktail sticks (toothpicks)
8 red ribbon bows
spoon with decorative handle

1 Split the cake and fill with butter icing. Place on the board and brush with apricot glaze. Cover with marzipan then red fondant, extending it over the board. Brush the lower edge of the cake with water. Roll the rest of the red fondant into a thin rope to go round the cake. Lay around the base of the cake and cut off the excess. Mark with a spoon handle. Dry overnight.

2 Roll out the white fondant to a 25cm/10in circle and trim neatly. Lay this icing over the cake and quickly drape 'cloth' over wooden cocktail sticks at eight equal positions around the cake.

3 Mark a 10cm/4in circle in the centre of the cake. Using a template of the small flower design, transfer to the cake with a needle. Press a fine knitting needle or skewer into the fondant to make the flowers. The red colour should show through – do not press quite so deeply for the stems and leaves.

4 Mark the child's name in the centre and pipe with a no. 0 tube.

5 Stick on the bows with a dab of royal icing. With a no. 2 plain tube and white royal icing pipe around the circle in the centre. With a no. I plain tube, pipe small dots around the edge of the cloth to finish.

COOK'S TIP
Bright red fondant is difficult to achieve at home because so much colour paste is needed. However, you can buy it from specialist shops; the bows can be found at department stores and cake shops.

Templates

The following templates, unless otherwise specified, are shown here at 50 percent of their actual size. Scale up to the size required on tracing paper or a photocopier before using.

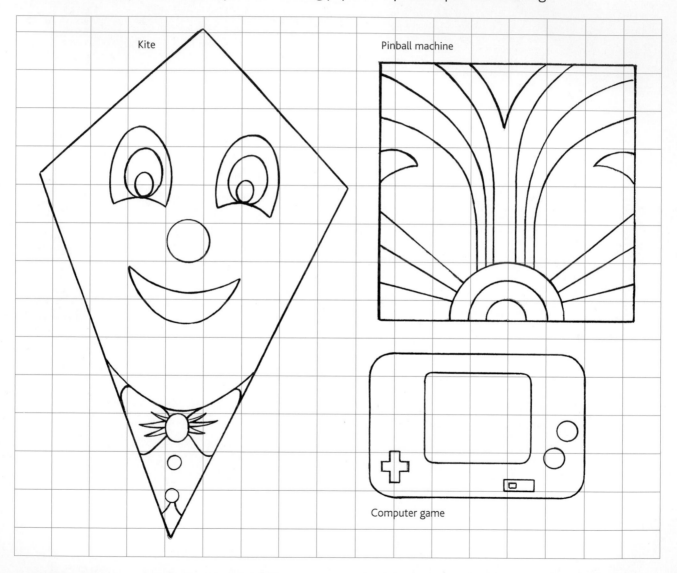

Kite

Pinball machine

Computer game

Fairy and
ballerina

Pirate's hat

Treasure map

Hickory dickory dock clock face

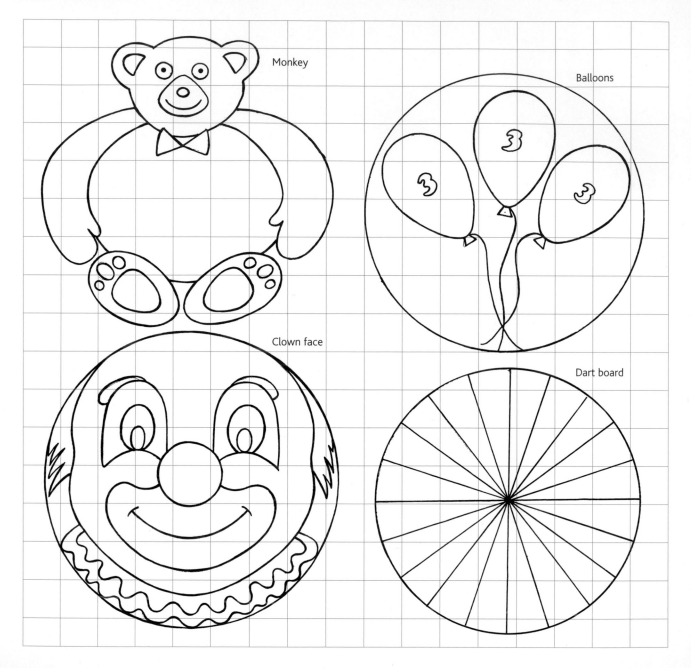

Monkey

Balloons

Clown face

Dart board

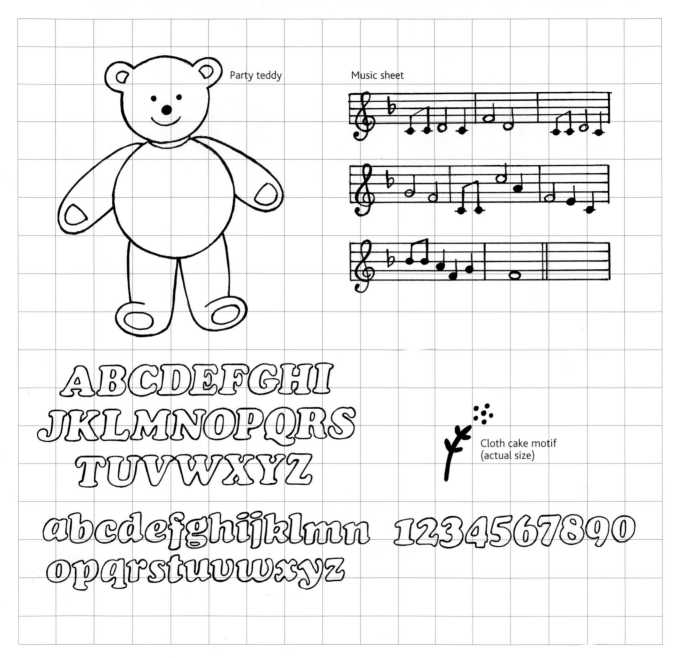

Party teddy

Music sheet

Cloth cake motif
(actual size)

Index